# Behind the Scenes
# Game Design

## JENNIFER HACKETT

**Children's Press®**
An Imprint of Scholastic Inc.

**Content Consultant**

Matthew Lammi, PhD

Assistant Professor, College of Education

North Carolina State University

Raleigh, North Carolina

Library of Congress Cataloging-in-Publication Data

Names: Hackett, Jennifer, author.

Title: Game design / by Jennifer Hackett.

Other titles: True book.

Description: New York : Children's Press, [2017] | Series: A true book

Identifiers: LCCN 2016057409 | ISBN 9780531235034 (library binding) | ISBN 9780531241462 (pbk.)

Subjects: LCSH: Computer games—Design—Juvenile literature. | Video games—Design—Juvenile literature.

Classification: LCC QA76.6 .H28325 2017 | DDC 794.8—dc23

LC record available at https://lccn.loc.gov/2016057409

SCHOLASTIC, CHILDREN'S PRESS, A TRUE BOOK™, and associated logos are trademarks and/or registered trademarks of Scholastic Inc., 557 Broadway, New York, NY 10012.

1 2 3 4 5 6 7 8 9 10 R 27 26 25 24 23 22 21 20 19 18

**Front cover: A soldier using a laptop**

**Back cover: A gamer playing**
***Angry Birds* on a smartphone**

# Find the Truth!

**Everything** you are about to read is true *except* for one of the sentences on this page.

Which one is **TRUE**?

**T or F**  The first video game designed specifically for entertainment was a tennis game.

**T or F**  All video games have a plot.

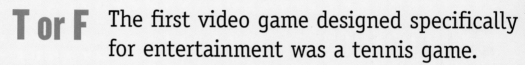

Find the answers in this book.

# Contents

## THE BIG TRUTH!

## Modeling in Three Dimensions

**An animated hero**

*Skylanders* toys

**Warning!**
Some of these projects use pointy,
sticky, hot, or otherwise risky objects.
Keep a trusted adult around to
help you out and keep you safe.

**A person playing
a game on a
smartphone**

# Press Start!

A girl in China jumps, dodges, and fights her way to hidden treasure. A boy in Jamaica puzzles out the final piece of a design challenge. Two friends in the United States clutch their controllers as they race around a twisting track. How is all this possible? Video games! Whether you're looking for excitement, challenge, or competition, there's something for everyone. From the moment you press Start, you're in for a whole world of wonder.

More than 180 million people in the United States play video games.

# Arcade Games

In the 1970s, before gaming **consoles** and computer games were widely available, people played games in arcades. Individual games were housed in boxes called cabinets. The cabinets had joysticks and buttons for the game and monitors, or screens, that displayed the action. Arcade games often featured simple goals, gameplay, and images. For example, *Pong* was a popular ping-pong-inspired game. It consisted of two moveable lines and a ball that bounced between them.

# A Timeline of Game Development

**3500 BCE**
People in Egypt play the oldest known board game, called senet.

**1958 CE**
A physicist at Brookhaven National Laboratory in New York develops *Tennis for Two*. It is the first video game made to entertain.

# Console and Computer Games

Nowadays, most video games are played on personal computers and gaming consoles such as Microsoft's Xbox or the Sony PlayStation. They often have detailed plots. Many popular games are parts of series, such as *The Legend of Zelda* or *Pokémon*. Games feature many different play styles. Some have players see action through a character's eyes. Others give players a birds-eye view. Many games connect to the Internet, so many players use them at once.

## 1972

The first home game console, the Magnavox Odyssey, is released.

## 1975

Atari's *Pong* is available to play at home for the first time.

## 1996

The Nintendo 64, the world's first 3D game system, is released in the United States.

9

# Mobile Games

Tablet computers and smartphones have opened up the gaming experience to new frontiers. Thanks to these pieces of technology, people can play video games wherever they are. Many popular mobile games, such as *Angry Birds*, mimic traditional arcade games. Other **genres** include sports, racing, adventure, and puzzle games. Big companies create some games. Others are the product of individuals designing their own games and apps.

*Angry Birds* was specially designed for devices with touchscreens.

# THE EVOLUTION OF CONTROLS

Game controls have come a long way. The first games used slides, switches, dials, buttons, or joysticks. These were generally part of the console or cabinet itself. The first handheld controllers were connected to the console by wire. By the 1980s, they regularly featured combinations of buttons, joysticks, arrows, and triggers. Wireless versions came in the 2000s, with some doubling as imaginary rackets, bats, and other equipment. Soon, we may not need physical controllers at all. Players of the future may control games with their minds!

**Buttons**

**Joysticks**

**Arrows**

Genre can affect everything from character design to color scheme.

# CHAPTER 2

# Types of Games

There are a lot of choices to make when creating a video game! Deciding what genre your game belongs to can help make those choices easier. Different genres have different gameplay. For example, a space-themed game in which the player earns points for zapping aliens would be very different from a racing game that takes place in space. Some games even fit into more than one genre!

← Released in 2016, *I Am Setsuna* was designed to remind players of 1990s role-playing games.

# The Journey to Win

Action-adventure is the most common video game genre. Popular action-adventure games include *Super Mario Bros.* and the LEGO series. Designers of these games create fantasy worlds that are full of surprises and obstacles. The games feature a cast of characters that help (or harm) players as they advance through each level and earn points and prizes. Players must use different tactics to survive and beat the game.

*Super Mario Bros.* became an instant classic action-adventure game when it was released in 1985.

## "Role-playing game" is often shortened to RPG.

## Character Quest

Role-playing games let players customize characters that grow stronger over the course of the game. Think of the classic *Pokémon* games. As you battle, your Pokémon get stronger. You can choose which new skills they learn. Some RPGs even allow players to create their characters from scratch. You can name them, choose what they look like, and more. Throughout the game, you can make choices such as what quests to accomplish when. RPGs often have many possible endings, too.

Some major sports series release updated versions of their games each year.

## Sports on the Screen

The very first video game made simply for entertainment was a sports game. It was called *Tennis for Two*. Today, the genre has grown to include major series such as *FIFA Soccer* and *Madden NFL*. Many of these games feature real athletes and stadiums. People can compete as their favorite team. For team sports, players usually control one athlete at a time. The rest of the team acts using **artificial intelligence**.

# Need for Speed

Racing games such as *Gran Turismo* and *Mario Kart* pit several players against one another in a dash to the finish line! Game designers pick what kind of vehicle players will race—cars, bikes, horses, planes, or even fictional vehicles. Designers also create all the twists, turns, hills, and obstacles of the racecourse. These can be simple loops or exciting trips through outer space or down a volcano.

**Many racing games allow players to customize their vehicles.**

# Puzzle and Strategy

Puzzle games from *TETRIS* to *Bejeweled* test logic and problem-solving skills. These games may not have characters or a story. Instead, they are all about solving puzzles that become increasingly difficult. Some games, such as *Age of Empires*, require a player to carefully think out every action in advance. These are games of **strategy**. It takes planning to create a challenging puzzle or strategy game! Designers must stay one step ahead of their smartest players.

Puzzle games such as *Candycrush* have simple gameplay but increasingly challenging puzzles.

An Afghan air force pilot uses a flight simulator to practice her skills.

# Simulation

Some games re-create parts of real life, such as farming or flying an airplane. These are **simulator** games. The first step in making a simulator is deciding what activity to turn into a game. Some of the most popular games of all time, such as *Sim City*, simulate daily life. Simulator games can even be used to train people to do an activity in real life, such as flying a space shuttle!

Noah Rosenfield and Danny Rivera work on their game, *Tilt*.

# Game On!

Creating a video game is no easy task. It often takes a team to build a game that is both fun and functional. First, game designers choose what platform the game will be played on and what type of game it will be. They brainstorm ideas for the game's setting, and characters. They also decide on the game's **mechanics**. Artists, writers, **programmers**, and others work with them to turn these ideas into reality.

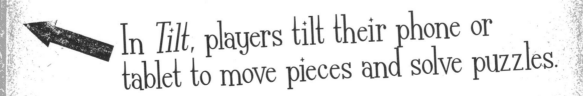

In *Tilt*, players tilt their phone or tablet to move pieces and solve puzzles.

A setting such as a spaceship can present unique challenges to a player.

# Setting the Scene

A game's environment can be as simple as a maze or as detailed as an entire fictional kingdom. The land, sky, and living things, and other objects all make up the game's environment. This setting is like the set of a play and an obstacle course at the same time. It determines what actions the player needs to do to move forward in the game.

# Choosing Characters

Characters, or avatars, represent the player in the game. Sometimes players design their own avatar. In other games, players take on the role of a preexisting character, like Super Mario. Game designers and artists work together on an avatar's appearance. For example, a cartoon style makes for a lighthearted game. A realistic character design gives the game a more dramatic and serious tone.

A designer creates a video game version of Indianapolis Colts team member Frank Gore for a football game.

# Making a Storyboard

Storyboards are sketches or illustrations that show the sequence of events in a game. They help artists and writers see how a game changes as the player advances through each level. For a simple game, there might be only a few sketches in the storyboard. A complicated game with many different possible story paths could have hundreds!

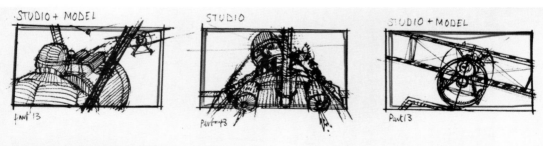

**Storyboards help designers chart out exactly how a game will work.**

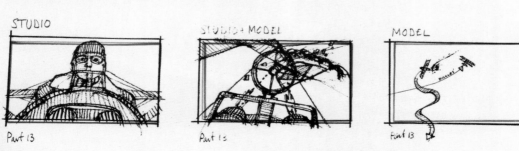

A character attacks an enemy.

# Putting It in Motion

Many game designers create their characters on a computer. They build three-dimensional, or 3D, models, using special software. Animators can make the models run, jump, fight, and do many other actions. The movements programmed into a character determine the movements a player can do. For example, animators create a jumping movement and a landing movement. This allows players to see their characters jump from an object and land on the ground.

Good code keeps all parts of a game running smoothly.

# Creating the Script

Once all of the big decisions have been made about the game, it is time to bring it to life. Game designers write a **code** that tells the system what to do and when to do it. A game's code is a special language of symbols and word combinations that computers understand. It's like a script that all parts of the game follow. This includes the characters, environment, dialogue, music, and so on. As the designers work, they decide on a lot of the little details that help support the big decisions.

# RANDOM BATTLES

Imagine you come across an enemy in a game and decide to attack. What happens? If the result of your attack seems random, it is! Random number generators decide if you hit or miss. It's similar to rolling dice. The game picks a random number called a seed. This determines the value of your attack. Another seed decides the value of your enemy's reaction. Whoever has the higher number wins!

1,024

652

# Modeling in Three Dimensions

**To bring a 3D character to life, a game designer creates a 3D model in a computer program.**

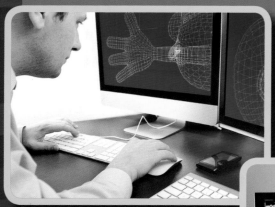

The model begins as a set of basic geometric shapes such as spheres, cylinders, or rectangular boxes. The shapes make up the core of a character. Because the shapes are simple, they're easy to move and pose.

Sometimes the position and movement of these shapes are based on the movements of actors wearing special suits. The suits are marked so a camera can track the various parts of the actors' bodies.

Details such as color and texture are added over this skeleton to create a finished character.

# Cutting-Edge Creations

Video games have come a long way since they were invented back in the 1950s. Television sets, computers, consoles, and mobile devices are constantly being improved and updated. These advancements are giving game designers unique ways to test the limits of their imagination and creativity. As new technology continues to emerge, gamers around the globe are eager to be a part of that adventure.

In 2017, about 30 percent of all game developers were working on virtual reality games.

# Going Inside the Game

Virtual reality is one type of technology that has many game designers and gamers excited. Virtual reality makes games more **immersive**. Players wear headsets that shut out the real world and display the game on screens in front of the players' eyes.

Game designers have also brought immersive games into the real world. These games augment, or add to, reality. For example, *Pokémon GO* players visit real places and use their phones to find virtual objects within them.

# RESEARCH AT PLAY

Scientists sometimes need to work through large amounts of **data**. They can get millions of people to help out by turning their research into a game! One example is *Planet Hunters*. The game explains what researchers are looking for in their data. The player then hunts for anything that matches that description. It's like playing a game of I spy. The players have fun and become citizen scientists.

# Interactive Games

Interactive games are designed to work alongside real toys. Designers create both a physical and a digital, or computer, version of characters or objects. When the physical toy is used with the game, it unlocks new levels, characters, or items. This means designers can constantly create new items a user can play with both in the game and in real life.

Interactive games such as *Skylanders* bring toys to life.

Games such as *Minecraft* create endless opportunities for players to design and build.

## Players as Creators

Some of the most popular games, such as *Minecraft* and *Super Mario Maker*, don't have a story or set environment. Instead, they provide players with the building blocks to create their own worlds or levels. Players can make elaborate structures or complicated game levels that they can then share online.

These activities can give players a taste of what game design is like. Do you feel inspired? The future of game design could be you! ★

# Think Like a Designer

Long before a video game is made, its designers make a series of decisions about what the game will be like. Try this activity to plan your own video game. Then make a prototype, or trial version, out of paper and test your game.

## What You Need

- ☐ notebook paper
- ☐ markers or colored pencils
- ☐ butcher paper
- ☐ notebook
- ☐ construction paper
- ☐ coins, buttons, or other small objects

**THINK AHEAD**

Before a game is made, its makers need to know how it will be played and what it will do. What would happen if a designer started to make a game without a plan?

# ★ **What to Do** ★

**1.** Decide what kind of game you want to make. Will it be a puzzle game? Action-adventure? Remember, each genre has different gameplay.

**2.** Brainstorm the different settings and the types of characters you would like to include in your game.

**3.** Write down the goal that you want the player to achieve. Plot out how the player will progress in the game.

4. Create a paper prototype of your game. Pick one part of the game, such as one level of a puzzle game or one interaction in an action-adventure game. Now make a physical version of it. You might draw the puzzle on a piece of construction paper. Or you can make a game board.

# WHAT HAPPENED?

**A.** Your prototype represents your game's basic mechanics and appearance. What other features can you add to complete it as a video game?

**B.** What parts of your paper prototype would be controlled by computer coding in a video game?

**C.** What would the next steps be for a video game designer? How might their process be different?

**5.** Use coins, buttons, or other small objects to represent the players or movable parts in the game. The players can move through the game, interacting with challenges such as obstacles or enemies.

# THE
# TRUE ANSWER

Programmers combine backgrounds, characters, dialogue, music, and more to create a game. Code defines how all these elements work individually and in cooperation. This is a lot to fit together, so it helps to have a plan. Then programmers can make small fixes along the way, instead of trying to keep track of major changes in the code.

# Make a 3D Model

Storyboards are two-dimensional, or flat. Game designers turn these flat drawings into 3D characters. Game designers may create 3D models on computers, but you can create one with just a few supplies. Find out how these models make it easier to bring games to life.

## What You Need

- ☐ pencil
- ☐ paper
- ☐ modeling clay
- ☐ pipe cleaners or straightened paper clips

**THINK AHEAD**

Three-dimensional models simplify complicated shapes such as hands and faces. This makes them easier to move and change. Look at yourself in the mirror. What geometric shapes do you see? Imagine making a model of your face. Would it be easier to make an exact copy of yourself or to use basic geometric shapes?

# What to Do

**1.** Draw or find an image of a person you want to model.

**2.** Create a table that lists the shapes you will use to make each part of your character. Here's an example:

| BODY PART | SHAPES |
|-----------|--------|
| Arm | Cylinder, sphere |
| Torso | Rectangular box |

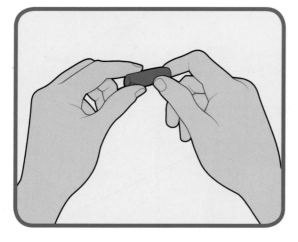

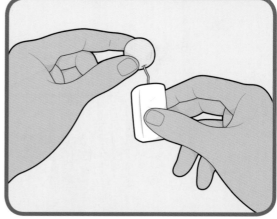

**3.** Using the modeling clay, start making each shape you listed in the chart.

**4.** Connect your geometric shapes together using pipe cleaners or straightened paper clips. These wires are flexible, so your model will be able to move. Use one paper clip or pipe cleaner for each body part.

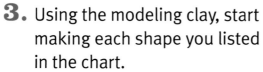

# WHAT HAPPENED?

**A.** Would it be easier or more difficult to make a more detailed model? Why or why not?

**B.** How difficult is it to change aspects of the model, such as the size, position, or shape of different parts?

**C.** Why might a game designer want to make a simple character model before making a more detailed one?

**5.** Add details such as props, facial expressions, or even clothing.

**6.** Move your model into various positions. Can you make it look like it's running or celebrating? What about sad or angry?

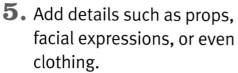

# THE
# TRUE ANSWER

**Starting simple makes it easier for game designers to make small—or large—adjustments without losing hours of work creating and replacing small details. They break characters down into basic geometric shapes to make 3D models. Computer programs allow them to see how different models move before adding details. Once designers are happy with their simplified models, they add in details to make a finished character ready for an adventure.**

# True Statistics

**Global revenue from video games in 2016:** More than $90 billion

**Percent of gamers under 18 as of 2016:** 27

**Percent of households in the United States that play video games as of 2016:** 63

**Number of people who work together to make a video game on average:** 1–100s

**Percent of people who play video games with friends or family as of 2016:** 54

**Percent of people who mainly play games on their smartphones as of 2016:** 36

**Number of people around the world who play video games as of 2016:** 1.8 billion

Did you find the truth?

**T** The first video game designed specifically for entertainment was a tennis game.

**F** All video games have a plot.

# Resources

## Books

Ceceri, Kathy, and Mike Crosier (illustrator). *Video Games: Design and Code Your Own Adventure: With 17 Projects*. White River Junction, VT: Nomad Press, 2015.

Hansen, Dustin. *Game On! Video Game History from Pong and Pac-man to Mario, Minecraft, and More*. New York: Feiwel & Friends, 2016.

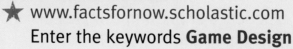

**Visit this Scholastic website for more information on game design:**
★ www.factsfornow.scholastic.com
Enter the keywords **Game Design**

# Important Words

**artificial intelligence** (ahr-tuh-FISH-uhl in-TEL-uh-juhns) the ability of computers and robots to perform tasks that normally need human intelligence, such as being able to understand speech and make decisions

**code** (KODE) the instructions of a computer program, written in programming language

**consoles** (KAHN-sulz) computers designed specifically to play video games

**data** (DAY-tuh) collected information

**genres** (ZHAHN-ruhz) particular kinds of creative work

**immersive** (i-MUR-siv) completely absorbing or surrounding

**mechanics** (muh-KAN-iks) the ways in which a program or machine operates

**programmers** (PROH-gram-urz) people whose job is to write computer programs, including games

**simulator** (SIM-yuh-lay-tur) a machine or program that allows you to experience or perform complex tasks digitally, without doing them in real life

**strategy** (STRAT-uh-jee) a plan for winning a battle or achieving a goal

# Index

Page numbers in **bold** indicate illustrations.

# About the Author

Jennifer Hackett studied physics and history at the College of William and Mary. After she decided she wanted to write instead of research, she attended New York University's Science, Health, and Environmental Reporting Program. She has written about space exploration, climate change, and cool technology, and currently works as Scholastic MATH's associate editor. She's played video games since she was three and loves Nintendo games.